D1460968

Comparing Minibeasts

Minibeast Homes

Charlotte Guillain

www.heinemannlibrary.co.uk

Visit our website to find out more information about Heinemann Library books.

To order:

☎ Phone +44 (0) 1865 888066

▤ Fax +44 (0) 1865 314091

▤ Visit www.heinemannlibrary.co.uk

Heinemann Library is an imprint of Capstone Global Library Limited, a company incorporated in England and Wales having its registered office at 7 Pilgrim Street, London, EC4V 6LB – Registered company number: 6695582

Heinemann is a registered trademark of Pearson Education Limited, under licence to Capstone Global Library Limited

Edited by Nancy Dickmann and Catherine Veitch
Designed by Joanna Hinton-Malivoire
Picture research by Elizabeth Alexander
Production by Duncan Gilbert and Victoria Fitzgerald
Originated by Heinemann Library
Printed and bound in China by South China Printing Company Ltd

ISBN 978 0 431 19492 9
14 13 12 11 10
10 9 8 7 6 5 4 3 2 1

British Library Cataloguing in Publication Data
Guillain, Charlotte.
Comparing minibeasts.
Homes.
592.1'564-dc22

Acknowledgements
We would would like to thank the following for permission to reproduce photographs: Alamy pp. **11** (© Roger Eritja), **12** (© Manor Photography), **20** (© Emir Shabashvili), **14** (© cbimages); Capstone Global Library pp. **18** (Steven Mead), **23 top** (Steven Mead); Corbis pp. **5** (© Theo Allofs/zefa), **16** (© William Radcliffe/Science Faction); FLPA p. **17** (© Konrad Wothe/Minden Pictures), Photolibrary pp. **4** (Don Johnston/All Canada Photos), **7** (Michael Fogden/OSF), **10** (Oxford Scientific), **8** (Paul Freed/Animals Animals), **9** (David M Dennis/Animals Animals), **19** (Clarence Styron/age footstock), **15** (Polka Dot Images), **23 middle bottom** (David M Dennis/Animals Animals); Shutterstock pp. **6** (© Styve Reineck), **13** (© David Lee), **21** (© Florin Tirlea), **22 top left** (© alle), **22 bottom left** (© Levitskiy Nikolay), **22 top right** (© aaaah), **22 bottom right** (© Eric Isselée), **23 bottom** (© Florin Tirlea), **23 middle top** (© David Hughes).

Cover photograph of a beehive reproduced with permission of Shutterstock (©Subbotina Anna). Back cover photograph of termite hills reproduced with permission of Shutterstock (© Styve Reineck).

The publishers would like to thank Nancy Harris and Kate Wilson for their assistance in the preparation of this book.

Every effort has been made to contact copyright holders of material reproduced in this book. Any omissions will be rectified in subsequent printings if notice is given to the publishers.

Contents

Meet the minibeasts 4

On and in the ground 6

On water 10

Wood 12

Plants 14

Webs and nests 16

How big? 22

Picture glossary 23

Index .24

Meet the minibeasts

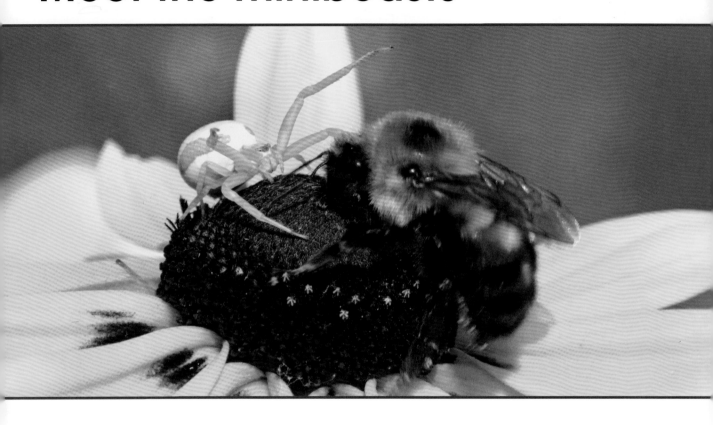

There are many different types
of minibeasts.

Minibeasts live in many different types of homes.

On and in the ground

Some termites build homes out of mud.

tunnels

Termites make tunnels in their homes.

Some centipedes live in soil.

Earthworms make tunnels in soil.

On water

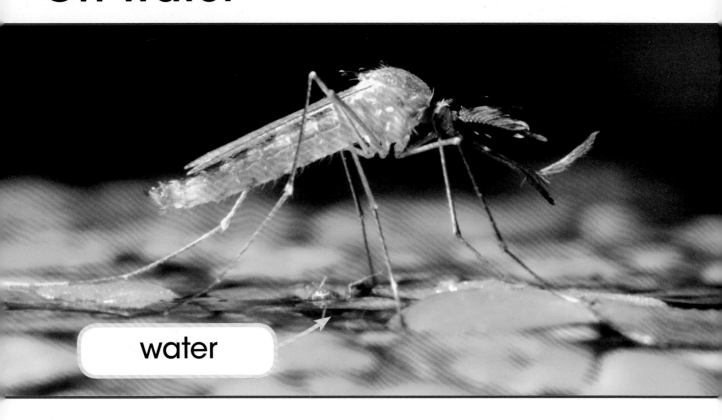

water

Some insects live on water.

eggs

Some insects lay their eggs in water.

Wood

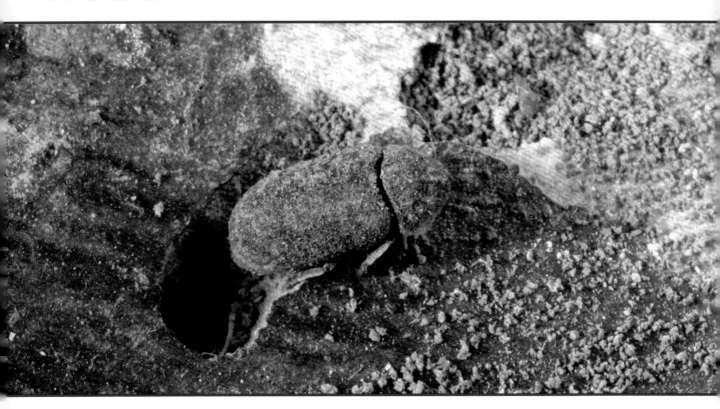

Many insects live in wood.

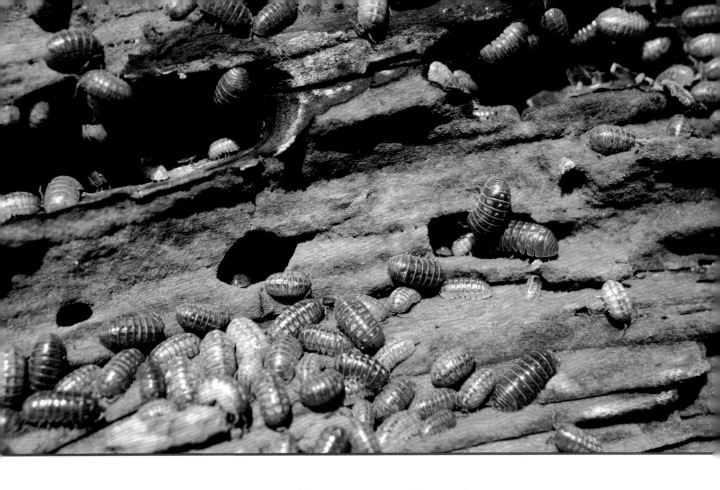

Many woodlice live under logs.

Plants

leaf

Some insects live on leaves.

stick insect

Some insects live in trees
and bushes.

Webs and nests

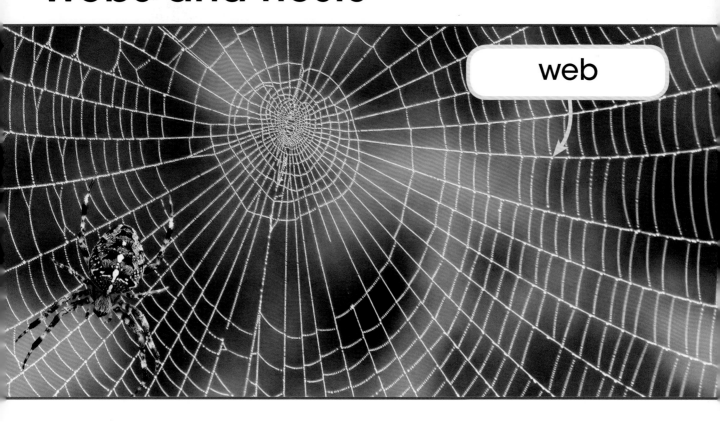

web

Spiders make webs from silk.

Some spider webs are like tunnels.

nest

Some caterpillars make nests from silk.

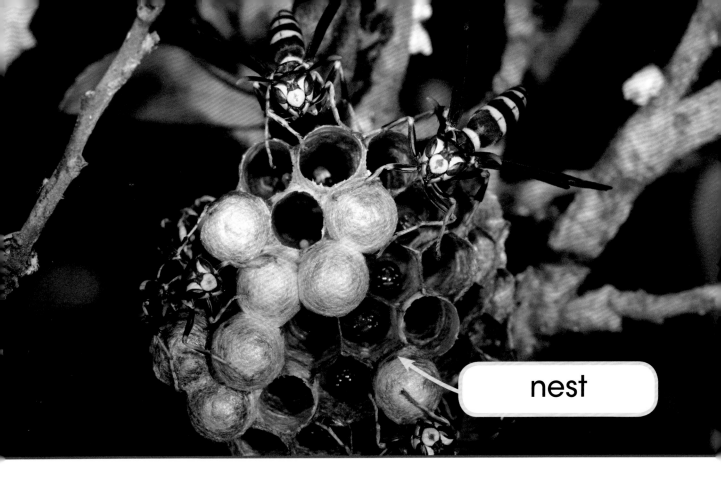

nest

Some wasps make nests from plants they eat.

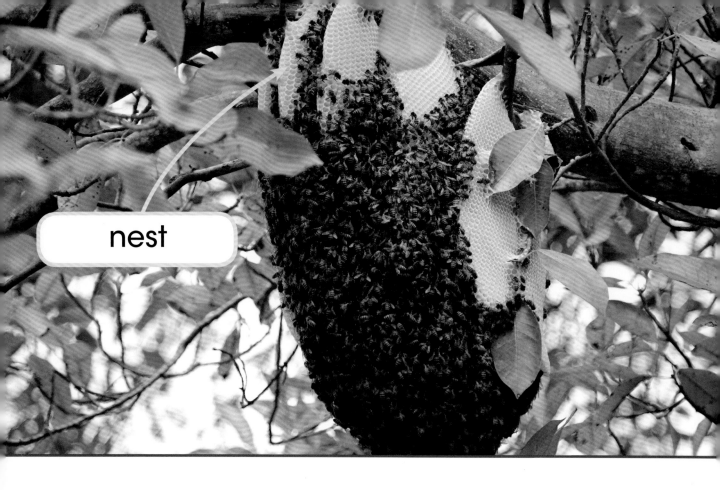

nest

Honeybees make nests out of wax.

The honeybees live in the nest.

How big?

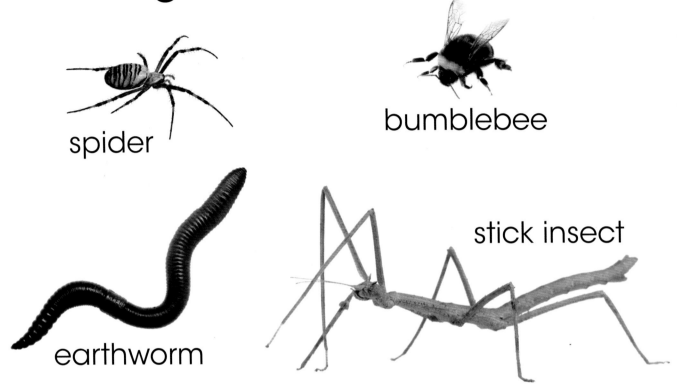

spider

bumblebee

stick insect

earthworm

Look at how big some of the minibeasts in this book can be.

Picture glossary

silk soft, strong material

soil top layer of ground that you can grow plants in

tunnel long underground passageway

wax sticky yellow material

Index

bush 15

leaves 14

log 12, 13

mud 6

nest 18, 19, 20, 21

soil 8, 9, 23

tree 15

tunnel 7, 9, 17, 23

water 10, 11

web 16, 17

Notes to parents and teachers

Before reading

Make a list of minibeasts with the children. Try to include insects, arachnids (e.g. spiders), crustaceans (e.g. woodlice), myriapods (e.g. centipedes and millipedes), earthworms, slugs, and snails. Ask the children if they know where any of these minibeasts live. What sort of homes do minibeasts make for themselves?

After reading

- Go on a hunt for spider webs – a good time to do this is on a misty morning. Where do spiders make their webs? Take photographs of the webs you find and look at them together on the interactive whiteboard. Look at the structure of the webs carefully. Try making a web together with string on the classroom wall. Is this easy to do?
- Take the children to hunt for other minibeasts. Help them to peel back bark on rotten logs, look under stones, look for worms in soil, or find caterpillars on leaves. Draw up tally charts with the children to record how many different places minibeasts were found.
- Read the children *The Very Busy Spider* by Eric Carle.